My Delight in My Beloved

My Delight in My Beloved

A Single Woman's Song of Songs

by Naomi M. Wong

RESOURCE *Publications* • Eugene, Oregon

MY DELIGHT IN MY BELOVED
A Single Woman's Song of Songs

Resource Publications
An Imprint of Wipf and Stock Publishers
199 W. 8th Ave., Suite 3
Eugene, OR 97401

www.wipfandstock.com

PAPERBACK ISBN: 978-1-5326-9337-3
HARDCOVER ISBN: 978-1-5326-9338-0
EBOOK ISBN: 978-1-5326-9339-7

Manufactured in the U.S.A.   AUGUST 14, 2019

To my family and friends, who hoped on my behalf
To my Lord and Love, by whom all things are made possible

Contents

Preface

MY DELIGHT IN MY BELOVED is best read cover-to-cover since it describes a linear narrative of the transformation that can take place in the presence of unconditional and unrelenting love. This narrative starts with "A Troubled Night" and ends with "Mutual Adoration", sections both inspired by sub-headings in some versions of *The Song of Songs*. Footnotes are included anywhere scripture is paraphrased, so that the reader may look up the references for further reflection. All scripture referenced comes from the New King James Version of the Bible. Although the New King James Version calls the biblical book "The Song of Solomon", I use the phrase "Song of Songs" in the title of this work in order to emphasize the greatness of God's love. Truly, there is none greater.

Introduction

Intimacy and the Troubled Night

IN THE GOSPELS, CHRIST asserts that abundant life can only be accessed through relationship with him.[1] Yet, after having said a prayer of commitment to the Lord, serving weekly in a community of believers, and taking fifteen minutes per day to read the Bible, we may still feel like something is missing. God, who does not lie, claims to be the source of our fulfillment. So, if we have accepted Christ into our hearts and still do not feel fulfilled, what are we missing? Common scapegoats for our dissatisfaction include lack of a stimulating job, lack of secure finances, and lack of a spouse or children. Meaningful work, financial security, and family are all blessings from God that add depth and richness to life. However, if Christ is to be believed, there is an intimacy that *is* true life, a knowledge that touches the innermost parts of our being, a relationship that can satisfy our deepest longing more than any thing or any person in the world.

How, then, do we access this life abundant, this unparalleled intimacy? There are myriad answers to such a question ranging from "do whatever strikes your fancy" to "fill the God-shaped hole with God". While my own convictions lean toward the latter, I believe that such platitudes merit some unpacking. I have found the book of *The Song of Songs* to be an edifying reflection in this respect.

The book of the Bible known as *The Song of Songs*, *The Song of Solomon*, or *Canticles* is arguably the boldest written description and proclamation of love in human history. It reflects in beautiful, multifaceted imagery the love between a man and a woman as well as the love between God and his people. Although *The Song of Songs* is typically reserved for ministering to married couples as a celebration of human sexuality, I have found that

---

1. John 10:7–10

the book engages matters of the heart that can also inform and direct the individual's search for intimacy with God.

My Delight in My Beloved begins with a section entitled, "A Troubled Night", which takes inspiration from passages in chapters 3 and 5 of *The Song of Songs*. While there is some uncertainty surrounding the events described in these Bible passages—whether they are dreams, fantasies, or actual events within the narrative of the song—it is safe to conclude that they express the deep yearning and emotional distress that can accompany intense desire. In both sections, the heroine, called the Shulamite, longs for her Beloved and searches for him. In Song of Songs 3:1–6, the Shulamite searches through the city at night and frantically inquires of the night watchmen as to whether they have seen her Beloved. The passage ends with her finding the Beloved, and she does not let him go until their love has been consummated.

In chapter 5:2–8, however, the Shulamite has a more disturbing experience. She hears the Beloved calling to her in the night. When she opens the door, though, he is gone. Once again, she goes out in search of him. Her search takes her through the dark city and ends with the night watchmen abusing her. The Shulamite charges the Daughters of Jerusalem to tell her Beloved that she is lovesick,[2] if they should come across him. Whether dream, fantasy, or reality within the song's narrative, these passages are reflective of common emotional events in the Christian life.

Although much of *The Song of Songs* is a jubilant celebration of love, I chose to start *My Delight in My Beloved* with "A Troubled Night" because so many Christians are familiar with that Troubled Night emotional space. Perhaps we once perceived Jesus calling to us, beckoning us with love. Perhaps we had known his love before. We had tasted and seen that he was good. Or, we had very much desired to experience him in that way. When he called to us, his voice was sweet to our ears. However, when we rose to open the door to him, we did not see him. Maybe we wandered, searching frantically, calling for him. In our search, we may have been ridiculed or abused, even. Maybe there was a particular situation in which we wished to see God intervene, and he did not follow through in the way that we had hoped.

This is the Troubled Night: to seek the Lord and to wonder if he is listening, if he cares, or if he has become inaccessible. The Troubled Night is about longing for the abundant life that Jesus offers. It is about the

2. Song of Solomon 5:8

disconnect that occurs in the space between the promise of deep, satisfying intimacy and the fulfillment of that promise. The Troubled Night is a time of lovesickness that may last for one literal night or for years and years' worth of nights.

As the biblical book of *The Song of Songs* comprises eight chapters in total, the last three being both jubilant and mildly blush-worthy, we can infer that the Troubled Night in chapter 5 is only a temporary setback for the Shulamite and her Beloved. In fact, at the end of that chapter, even in the heartache of not having found the Beloved, the Shulamite reflects on how wonderful he is.[3] In chapter 6, they are back at their exuberant love proclamations as if the Troubled Night had never occurred.

In this manner, reflecting on the very nature of the relationship between the lovers can bring hope of relief and restoration to the troubled soul. The Shulamite and her Beloved frequently convene to enjoy one another's presence and to invite the other to interaction. When the two are not in close physical proximity, they are reflecting on everything that they love about each other. They seem to be ever-inviting, ever-seeking, and ever-enjoying.[4]

Our Lord is ever-seeking and ever-inviting. He *wants* to be found by us that we may live in enjoyment of him and he of us. So, then, our search and invitation of him must be established in trust, in faith. In remembering everything we love about our Lord and how wonderful he is, faith can look like a simple, "What if . . . ?" This should not be done in the anxiety-ridden way of imagining worst-case scenarios, but rather a hopeful envisioning, "What if . . . ?"

What if unconditional love, understanding, the deepest kind of connection, and life abundant are available to every person? What if the love for which we have been waiting, longing, and searching actually exists? What if such a love is not found in a mere human or even in a community of humans, but in an everlasting, personal, attentive, compassionate source of living water?[5] What if he has been waiting for us, longing for us, and searching for us? What if he is right here beckoning to us with open arms?

3. Song of Solomon 5:10–16

4. Examples: Song of Solomon 2:2–13, 5:10–16

5. John 4:10

My invitation

I was in a long Troubled Night of my own when I heard, in prayer, the still small voice of our Lord say, "Come away." Although I was frustrated and near despondence, I came away both geographically and spiritually, setting aside special time to seek God in prayer every day. To be honest, I do not think I expected much from that time, but I carried with me a tiny, half-hearted hope, "*What if* he does something?"

During that time, I came before the Lord in prayer for an hour, sometimes two or three, every day. I cried a lot. I listened and waited. When I said anything to God at all, I expressed anger. It was all I knew to do. He had told me to come. So, I came and kept coming. Mysteriously, and only by our Lord's great mercy, my constant prayer of, "God, I'm mad at you" became, "God, I love you". For the remainder of that season, I spent my days writing love poems to him, and sometimes, when I listened, he spoke to me poems of his own! Thus, this book was formed, shaped, and birthed, even as I was transformed in the presence of our kind and loving Lord.

So now, I, along with my co-author and beloved friend, the author and finisher of our faith, invite the reader to ask, "What if?"

A note to single women in the church

I hope this book will speak to every reader, especially to those who love the Lord. However, single women are particularly on my heart. Single women in the church bear a striking resemblance to the Shulamite[6] in that we are loved by the Lord, but we often struggle to make our way among the other members of his bride. As church ministry is often geared toward married couples and families, single people can be made invisible, or worse, made to explain their presence and assert their relevance in the community. Single women in the community of Christ can be prone to Troubled Nights between the pressure to be married, the pressure not to look desperate for partnership, and the lack of resources for singles beyond a certain age.

My prayer for single women in the church is that our desire to seek the Lord will lead to vibrant, fulfilled life in Christ despite the slow-changing nature of the church's view on singleness. Equally importantly, I want to encourage my Christian sisters that we should not turn against each other because of the pressures we encounter in the church. In this book, I try to

6. Song of Solomon 1:5-6

shed some light on the power of words to build up or to tear down. Ultimately, I hope that we will learn to focus on our own relationships with the Lord and also to turn each other toward Christ.

My Delight in My Beloved is not meant to voice the concerns of all single women in the church. My intention, however, is that this book will give single women the dignity to search for deep intimacy in the unconditional love presence of our Savior and King. After all, *he* is the reason we are in his church. If Jesus invited us, we belong. His heart for us is only love, and his intentions are pure.

Come, enter in

Our God is an experienced lover who has nothing to prove to his loved ones. He sets us in a place of honor and lifts our faces to meet his gaze. He does not ravish us in his desire, but is gentle in his advances, patiently explaining when fear arises, reassuring with a gift of peace when going deeper hurts. Our intimacy is one of compassionate discipleship as he teaches us how to receive from him. Through respectful and kind interactions, he imparts life and healing to us. He is a sturdy arbor on which the tendrils of our fragile trust may climb, and in him, we find wholeness. He is thoroughly steadfast—and of good humor to boot!

What have we done to deserve such treasure?

"Nothing," our Lord of Grace whispers. "Just come to me."

Jesus, Lover of Our Souls, how exceedingly generous and kind you are! Take joy, our Lord and Love, in our worship. It is not much, but it is all we have to give.

A Troubled Night

The Woman

I waited for you
Screaming out for deliverance
Or your presence, at least
Through pain-filled days
And tormented nights
I waited and you did not show

When you called me away
To speak my mind
I had little to say other than tears
That resulted in bloody snot
I waited.
You said, "Some deliverance only happens through tears."

#

Longing

The despondent realization
That this is all life has to offer
Every new height

Plunges to a further depth
The warmth of thrill plummets
To chilly despair
This endless search
These restless legs
Wandering to escape
That never-ending itch
For no relief

If I'd only sought you

But what else could I want so much more
That having you can be "not enough"?
Shame, indignation, rage
That's me
Forbearance
That's you

#

You love me too much to give me what I want
In place of what I need
I need you
I just don't know what it means to have you
The heaving of my lungs and the tugging in my chest
Want to know

#

Waiting for you is like
Standing in line for the water fountain
Only I'm wishing you'd drink from me
I am dominated by the need to be used
Perhaps for the vain power of feeling
Valued, worthwhile, and desired
Pitiful, I know
My head knows you want me
And you always have

So, why this longing?

The Beloved

All that came before was not bad
Be assured, my love
Let me show you what I can do
With your passion
In my hands

Reassurance

The Woman

It is in the dead of winter
In the drear of gray afternoon's light,
To the soft, mumbling drizzles
Dripping apathetically from gift roof ridges,
When the warmth of a comforter
Truly comforts
A downtrodden and dormant heart,
And the precious silence of tears gently
Collected in a bottle[1] fills the room,
That out of only love that takes two to kindle
Passion is reborn
Out from under the wings
Of First Trust

The Beloved

I seek my wayward betrothed here
She hides her face, ashamed
For having been carried away, enslaved
By predatory masters who abused her

1. Psalm 56:8

4

They tore down my image in her
But I have sought her out
To restore and make her new

Come away, my love[2]
Come away

The Woman

With tears of joy
My Beloved receives me
He showers me with kisses
No questions asked, only
Will you trust me?
No judgment nor rebuke

Well, maybe a small
Loving chide

The Beloved

My dear of little faith,
Why did you doubt?[3]

The Woman

I am needy
Parched and aching
With desperate gulps I drink

2. Song of Solomon 2:10
3. Matthew 14:31

5

As one saved from death

I cling to his cup

Sucking, barely tasting

His goodness flows down

My heaving breast

Covering, redeeming

This ill-used vessel

With extravagant generosity

He gives himself

To me

The Beloved

I have loved you with an everlasting love[4]
You are My Delight

The Woman

I have found something special

And yet, my heart folds over it

Like a glorious secret

The love I have waited for all these years

Has been waiting for me, too

Now he calls and my joy paralyzes me

From the top of my head

To the bottoms of my feet

Out the tips of my fingers

And my shining face

4. Jeremiah 31:3

I accept!

But the words come slowly

And actions even more so

Every inch of me wants to shout it out

That rags have turned to riches

Shame to triumph

Anger to soft and tender love

He's been waiting for *me*!

(to her Beloved)

Be my first love again

I have forgotten what it means for you to fill me

Yet how empty I am for you

I have forgotten the roughness of love

Yet how durable I feel to try

I have forgotten your grip and your manner

Yet how I ache for your embrace

A taste has whet my appetite

How I long to be one with you!

Oh, be gracious to me as I wait.

The Beloved

The wait is over, my love

Come to me, now

And do not delay

The Woman

I nearly shed my skin in search of you
One touch from you sends my head spinning
Though I want more, more, more
Deep down, because I've been wronged before
I hope; I beg:
Please let this not just be a pleasure to my senses
But a transformation of my soul
Come live in me, deeper
Deeper

The Daughters of the Kingdom

Tell us what you mean by "deeper"
O sister, what does our King give you
That awakens this longing in your heart?

The Woman

Sweet substantial somethings
He whispers in my ear
Each loving word building up
The ruins of our lost city
How his kindness flows
So gently into every dry
And thirsty crevice!
This is a taste of fulfillment
This is the beginning
Of the end of longing

O sisters, rejoice at his heart!

\#

He whispers love to me and seals it
Like a kiss in my ear
Then, life bursts forth
Washing away those places
Roughened by bad names
And the mark of condemnation
Now unbound, my instinctual heart
Leaps frantically from my chest
Before I can stuff it back in
My Beloved reminds me
My great neediness
In him
Is strength[5]

The Beloved

Be not ashamed, love.

The Woman

Sometimes going deeper
Looks like tears and heartache
Wondering how high highs
Become such low lows

5. 2 Corinthians 12:9

And why love can hurt
Beyond comprehension

(to her Beloved)

What could I ever hide from you?
Pain is not so eloquent or tactful
So when you ask
It always comes back to:
I don't trust you
But I want to

\#

It is in this rawness
Of extending a vulnerable, wounded hand
And in the enfolding of the assuring hand
That sorrow, in security, pushes
Downward, inward, through
The pain crying out
If it's you, I want more
Deeper, deeper
Carving out the canyons
In preparation for
Floods of joy

The Beloved

I know you love me
Even when your heart is

Tattered beyond recognition

Your tears, your anger, your doubt

They don't scare me

I see the furtive adoration

In your lovelorn eyes

I hear the frustrated desire

In your accusing voice

"Betrayal" sprouts from misunderstanding

I know

You were made to be with me

And I will never give up on you

Love Renewed

The Woman

What wonders you work
On an open heart
In kindness bearing
With my bashful unveiling
What beauty you bring
From the tiniest bit of willingness
And with such gentleness
Your firm hands work
To cut the last ties
Of ill-gotten love
To make way
For fullness
Brimming, gushing, overflowing
To renewal

The Beloved

Look at my love
How she overflows
With life and abundance
Where once she wandered

The desert plains
Of heartache

My heart leaps when she lifts
Her gorgeous face in search
Of mine
Her smile radiant
Like her Father's heart

The Woman

When my Lord introduces me to his Father
Our Father claps him on the back, saying,
"Good job bringing this one home, son.
I've been waiting on my daughter a long time!"

Rejoice at his heart, all who hear!
Rejoice forevermore!

The Beloved

Lay back in my arms
And receive my love
The days of Fear are done
His reign has found its end
Come and drink me in

The Woman

What can I offer my King

Who owns the earth and the fullness therein[1]
Who owns the cattle on a thousand hills?[2]

What could I give to my Lord
Who supplies the very breath in my lungs
Who causes the sun to rise on me another day?

I wish to bring a precious gift to warm his heart

He bids me bring only what I am
"As is," he says

The Beloved

Don't spend time washing
When that's what I do
Don't worry that you're broken
I'm in the fixing business
And I just want you

The Woman

There is no safer place
Than these strong arms
That won't strong-arm me
In his embrace, I rest securely
My ear to his heart
His adoring gaze

1. Psalm 24:1
2. Psalm 50:10

Focused

Intently on my face

The Beloved

Keep coming, love

Even when self-hatred pulls you back

Even when there's snot mixed with your tears

And your hair might leave dirt smudges

On my feet

My feet don't mind

So, keep coming, love

Even when condemnation weighs you down

Even when your old ways take over

And you think I'm like an ordinary man

I'll turn your grime to gold

And your shame to praise

Just keep coming, love

I know you're bruised

But I won't break you

You're smoldering

But I won't quench you

I'm not afraid of your pain

Your urges, your doubts, your rage

My love, just keep coming

The Woman

Every inch of him
Vibrates with strength
Yet he handles the fragile heart
With tender care

He is glorious in holiness[3]
Righteousness bows down to him
Yet he embraces the unclean
And beckons the lame of spirit

His creation fits neatly
In the palm of his hand
Yet he makes himself small
To come and walk among us

O Daughters of the Kingdom, rejoice at his heart!

The Daughters of the Kingdom

We rejoice in him, sister!

The Woman to her Beloved

How will you make
This enclosed garden,
This shut-up spring,
This sealed fountain

3. Exodus 15:11

A fountain of gardens
And a well of living waters?[4]

The Beloved

I will open you
With tender words
And the kindest touch
For harsh words and actions
Have made you seal yourself away
But with my love, I'll draw you back

The Woman

Come open me, my Lord and Love
Reach through this constricting fear
Better yet, blow it all away
O mighty wind
For if the fragrance of my love
Is truly pleasant to you
Then, let these spices flow
Let my desire be sweet to you
And our garden enjoyable[5]

The Beloved

You have captured my heart
My love, My Delight

4. Song of Solomon 4:12
5. Song of Solomon 4:16

I find no spot in you[6]

You stand out among the billions

And my heart rejoices to hear your words

I am taken with you, love

And I'm all in

The Woman

I melt

In the warmth of his presence

His promise is secure

And his arms are steadfast

I flow surrendered into his stream

And patiently, he bears me along

The Beloved

I have you in the palm of my hand

And no mere man can change that

I've got all of who you are

Inscribed on my hand[7]

And I'm not giving you up

Not now, not ever

I love you, My Delight

I love you with all of my heart

The Woman

My mind can never comprehend

6. Song of Solomon 4:7
7. Isaiah 49:16

How from this despondent sludge

He's drawn up a crystal clear geyser

How life has exploded

From this barren wasteland

And yet, my heart knows well

That my Lord visits the poor in spirit

In due time

And in his good pleasure

He heals even those

Who are ignorant of their maladies

Just because he can

The Banner of Love: A Battle

The Beloved

How I long for you to call me "Love"
And not just "Lord"
I am ruler of all
King of kings, yes, and Lord of lords[1]
Your rock and your redeemer[2]
But I give myself to you, love
My very self

If I wanted a sniveler to do my bidding
I could have made a fleet of them
But I made My Delight
My beautiful treasure of great price
I have bought you back from your abusers
But I do not covet their role in your life

Of power and authority, I am beyond rich
But of your trusting friendship
I am intensely desirous

1. Revelation 19:16
2. Psalm 19:14

Your confidence in my good will
Is worth eternity

The Woman

He is gracious and patient
Yet all the more loving in his severity
For he loves us too much to leave us
Broken, naked, and blind
It's just that fixing can be painful
New clothes can be uncomfortable
And the senses can be overwhelming
Sensitive to our weaknesses
He half-carries, half-drags us
To the next baby step

The Daughters of the Kingdom

Come, sister, why do you tarry?
How can you waste your day
In isolation and in secret?
Surely your Beloved will wait
For you, an hour or so, at least
Come away and speak with us

The Woman

I cannot abide the thought
Of missing my time with him
How my heart longs just to be

Unveiled in his presence

My desire overwhelms me

And I am drawn to tears

At the dreadful obstacle of

Time

Between me and my Beloved

The Daughters of the Kingdom

The King is fair and good

He is glorious and immaculate

And cannot abide unrighteousness

He is all holy and in his presence

No one can stand

The Woman

Lord, forgive me when I shrink back

And when I cannot maintain eye contact

What glorious freedom you offer me!

Yet when I'm with you

My heart is so open

And I am so desirous

I fear I'll be overcome

With the wrong kind of ecstasy

The Beloved

You are changed in my presence, love

And yes, it may all happen in steps

But be patient with the process
I am pleased with your love
When you open your heart to me
These other things, the old ways,
Will pass away in my presence

Sit with me and drink me in
Be transformed to my likeness
Deceptions are powerless to my truth
And the only way they have power
Is if they keep you from me

The Woman

My Lord is so perfect
His love is so sweet
What power is in his kindness
And compassion in his touch!
No goodness can match his
No love can give him honor
The honor he is due
My love, to him, can only be filthy rags
My desire, simple dirt crumbles

The Beloved

How forlornly she sits
And bitterly she weeps
Not knowing the gift
That has been given to her:

Streams of living water

Springing up to eternal life[3]

Life with me

\#

My love is perfect in me

Not that she doesn't

Have room to grow

But she is spotless

I have made her so

I am righteous, full of mercy[4]

And I will let her know

The Woman

I am undone

For how can I love him

In my imperfection

But, indeed, how can I not?

No peace is true peace without him

No joy true joy

No life is life without my Love

What can a wretched soul do?

The Beloved

Sing to me, My Delight

3. John 4:14
4. Psalm 116:5

Turn your passion into song

It is sweet to my ears

My heart soars

When I hear your voice

Proclaiming love for me

Leave the old ways behind

Choose me again and again

And love me with all

Your heart, soul, mind, and strength[5]

The Woman

O Lord, you are rich in mercy

And your compassion abounds[6]

If you can do something

With this wild little heart

I beg you: help me!

Brother, Friend, King, and Love

May my desire for you be holy

My outpouring unquenched

My reception whole-hearted

And cleansed by your grace

Teach me your way, O Lord

Help me to walk in a smooth path[7]

5. Luke 10:27
6. Psalm 145:8
7. Psalm 27:11

The Beloved

If I love you back
(And I always have)
We will work things out
Do not fall into this trap
Of cleaning before coming
Just come

The Woman

What will you do with this tattered heart?
Every time you pour love in
It seeps right back out again

The Beloved

Love is wasteful
But it is never wasted
So when I pour into your heart
And love flows out
Through the cracks
Rejoice!
For everywhere it has touched
Is being healed, and
There's more where that came from!

The Woman

My King is close
In humbleness he tarries

Enjoying every moment
Of this loving suspense

To him, the abstinence
Is part of the consummation
Waiting with hopeful desire
Is love that purifies

The Beloved

My Delight is a snowdrop
Blossoming in the cold of winter
Pure and smooth
Dazzlingly brilliant is she
Her gaze is downcast
Her petals sealed, by nature,
Yet, by love, shall I lift her head
And cause her to be opened
When she shows her face
I shall be glad
And when she sends forth
Her fragrance
I shall rejoice

The Woman

Your love is like the morning dew
That falls in the silent hours
Between slumber and wakefulness
I awake with your mist

Delicately nestled in my lashes
Lingering preciously
Like echoes of promises whispered
In the dead of night
Just loud enough
For my longing heart to hear

The Beloved

Come to me and I will clothe you
In strength and honor[8]
My love, my fair one[9]
Do not shy away
I am going to help you
Not harm you, shame you, or judge you
Come to me, my love

The Woman

I've been the unattainable sex object before
And the plaything of many lustful imaginations
So now, kind words sting
As heartbreak finally catches up with me
And the long-abandoned hope of requited love
Expands in my tight and unsuspecting heart

Here my Beloved beckons me
And it is right and good

8. Proverbs 31:25
9. Song of Solomon 2:10

My heart gives way like a broken dam

Good tears, I suppose

The Beloved

My love, My Delight, why don't you turn to face me?

The Woman

I wish to greet my Beloved

With a beaming face, unstained by tears

I cannot stop shuddering

As I try to hold the goodness of his truth

Inside

The Beloved

Fear not, I have redeemed you[10]

The Woman

When my Beloved holds me

Everything else fades away

As I rest on him,

His life seeps into me

My mind is at rest

My spirit fulfilled

My body restored

When I lay back against him

Feeling the beating of his heart

10. Isaiah 43:1

And the warmth of his life

I am complete

(to the Daughters of the Kingdom)

O sisters, rejoice at his heart!

He will not use me

He prefers to tend me

Rather than to dominate

In our partnership,

He invites me

Yes, for the sake of others,

But also to help me to grow

#

My sisters look sideways at me

It is what they don't say

That hurts so much

The Beloved

Have a little faith, my love

Look at me and not at them

Touch my face and my smile

Feel my heart in yours

And know my good intention

Toward you

I will not harm you

I have given you a future

And a hope[11]

The Woman

I adore you, my Beloved
Your regard is unalterable
For you see all things
As they are
Your words are piercing
They cut right through
Deception and manipulation
Your strength is unparalleled
In your mighty presence
Every other power is undone
Your compassion is steadfast
Though no one can stand before you
You kneel to commune with us

I adore you, my Lord and my Love
How I adore you!

The Daughters of the Kingdom

She calls the King of kings her "Love"
And pours out her secondhand adoration
In a pool at his feet

11. Jeremiah 29:11

31

The Woman

My outpouring is less than perfect
But I must sing of my Beloved,
Praise his character, adore his heart
It is solely out of need and love
For my Lord that I speak thus
To my King

The Beloved

Do not be amazed
When people are in awe of you
Or even jealous
I created you to strike
Beauty and amazement
Into the heart of creation
That all might turn their heads
To their creator in praise

The Woman to the Daughters of the Kingdom

Come, sisters
See how he adores me
His eyes never part from my being
His heart is interwoven with mine
I am His Delight
He invites me to his House of Wine
Not through merit, but through grace
He anoints me at his table

And feeds me tasty things[12]
Look at this banner he places
Over me; it is his love[13]

Come, sisters
His love for me is non-negotiable
But there is room at the table
If you'd like to sit with us
Your opinion of me will never
Change his mind
But if you'd take your claws
Out of my flesh for a moment
You might just find your heart
Softened by his love and learn
Also to receive mine

12. Psalm 23:5
13. Song of Solomon 2:4

Restoration

The Woman

I have never known desire to be anything
Other than self-gratifying and ravenous
Sometimes it was violent and condemning
So, I'm not used to this kind and attentive
Gentle, tender, and giving love
How patient you are with me!

The Beloved

My Delight
You are all fair
There is no spot in you[1]
How you dazzle!
A queen among queens
The brightest of my stars
The jewel of my eye

The Woman

His love echoes through the space

1. Song of Solomon 4:7

Where condemnation used to penetrate me
I tense up, remembering how good feelings
Once led to bad results
Deception, mostly.

The Beloved

Receive, my love. Receive from me.

The Woman

With the release of breath
Tension fades to trust
Relaxation permits his hand to enter
My heavily guarded wound
Untouched by time, unseen by men
Pain melts into sadness
And sadness into vulnerability
In fragile desire, I fall open
Only to find I am already filled
For he has joined me in my wound
Saying, "Even here, you are not alone."

The Beloved

You are mine
In the way hearts are
When they are freely given
Not seized
And I am yours

In the way I AM

Extravagant love, constantly outpouring,

Unconditional

The Woman

I trustingly stay open

And his words wash through

One "I love you" after another

Building from enjoyment to ecstasy

"I will never leave you," he says.

He holds me in the palm of his hand

For once, I am fulfilled

And despite deep satisfaction,

I am safe

(to the Daughters of the Kingdom)

O Daughters of the Kingdom, rejoice at his heart!

For he will never leave me

The Daughters of the Kingdom

Her heart is one with his

They are intertwined

And they cannot be separated

The Woman

My Beloved is near to me

He has made himself found

In my presence
And I am found in his

The Beloved

I rejoice, my love. I rejoice!
We are together forever!

The Woman

Your words restore my life
You fill me with wonderful thoughts
By your good pleasure
You tell me you're healing me
And you do it by holding me
By your good pleasure
I am made whole

The Beloved

I will connect all the disjointed pieces
So that your head and your heart will agree
When I kiss your ears with truth
Your head will know and your heart be glad
And when I whisper love into your heart
Your head will be delighted in me

The Woman

You make me laugh, my Lord and Love
And laughter does me good

Especially in this time of rewiring
When sorrow mingles with joy
Pain, comfort, and ecstasy are
Yet to be detangled
And love is being redefined

The Beloved

I draw you gently, My Delight
I draw you gently with bands
Of love[2]
Not to be my slave or toy
But to be my friend
And *my* beloved

The Woman

You love me to tranquility
Rather than to enfeeblement
The kindness of your words
Overtakes me and I give in
Not helpless nor powerless
Only most peacefully
Surrendered in trust
To one I know is trustworthy

The Beloved

You never knew words could be so powerful, did you?

2. Hosea 11:4

Just imagine how all those evil words tore you down

You were under them for many years, so please

Give yourself a little grace on this journey

Soak yourself in my words

Immerse yourself in my heart

And I will not only heal you, but

I will restore you beyond the original

To glory and grace[3]

My love and My Delight

That is what I will do for you

The Woman

He takes his special bottle

And bringing it to my cheek

He says, "This is for happy tears, too."

The Beloved

We are one, my darling

We are one:

I in you and you in me[4]

So, do not let others

The conniving and condemning

Voices

Convince you otherwise

You are clean

3. Psalm 84:11
4. John 15:4

Because of the word I've spoken
To you[5]
I am yours and you are mine[6]

The Woman

He touches my wounds with knowing hands
Expert precision, just the right pressure
As the pain of abandonment rips through
The delicate scar tissue of time, I shriek

The Beloved

You are strong, my love

The Woman

I know my longing is for him
Though I'd settle for a bit of numbness
My Love desires more on my behalf
He walks me through the agony
Toward healing

The Beloved

Why do you cling to me so tightly?
Relax a little and you will see
These arms are wrapped around you
And I will never, ever let you go

5. John 15:3
6. Song of Solomon 2:16

The Woman

I am shaken by abandonment
Alone with the horror of my past
Unwanted

Touch me
So I may remember your desire
Fill me, please

The Beloved

You sense an unrecoverable loss
And you have given up
Hope of healing

But watch me!
Watch me give you what no one can
Watch me teach you what you long to know
Watch me give you the desires of your heart

#

I will fill your empty space, my love
But first of all, I will heal you
Take the time to let me work
And do not stuff achievement
Into your wound
Trust me, love

The Woman

This is my trust

Raw, bare, vulnerable

I have no safeguard

In coming to give you

All that I am, inside and out

Let the lovely places of my soul

Be pleasant to you, Lord

Receptive to your love

And to your life

The Beloved

Patience, my love

Your desires are good

But we must not rush

I want more of me in you, too

You want to hold nothing back

Which is admirable

I will give you your desires

In due time

The Woman

You are the kindest one

I have ever met

And that is why I give myself to you

You don't bend or change to please me

And your mercy is a pair of pruning shears

When necessary

Though I encounter you
I do not know you
Not as well as I wish to, anyway
I just know that you're good
And that's why I want more of you
In me

The Beloved

My Delight hides her beautiful face
Out of fear and shame, she does this
But I will shine my light
Upon her countenance
I will transform her sight
And cause the world to see her
As she is
In me

Oneness Teaching Wholeness

The Woman

O Lord, my Love
If there is anything I have kept back
Bring it to the forefront
Though I will to be open
My heart seems to have shut down
But your love is stronger
Than my protective instincts
Your love *is* my protection

The Beloved

You're afraid to know me more
Because you believe grace is
Too good to be true
You're afraid I'll turn into a monster
Like the others did. Will you trust me?
My love for you has never changed
And it never will

The Woman

I have holes, paradoxes
They are large and gaping
While quite tight and tender
I have these spaces
Once filled with desire,
Idolatry, even for good things
I'm glad those things are gone
Come and fill me, I beg you!

The Beloved

Do not be dismayed, my love
This emptiness will not destroy you
I am already at work
Healing you, so I can fill you
I will not leave you empty forever
Trust me

The Woman

He gives and gives and gives to me
My heart is overwhelmed in his grace
His words soften me
He will not shove his way in
But as I open, his sweetness enters
And peace follows after, permeating
Every aching inch of me

(to her Beloved)

Lord, deliver me from myself
From this propensity to insert
The flesh
Into space consecrated by
The Spirit
Make me alive in your presence
Exuberant in your passion
Connected in body, soul, and mind
Unencumbered by sinful
Weakness

The Beloved

I am not afraid of your sinfulness
And I know your affection is sincere
Albeit incomplete
I'll see your infatuation and raise you
My everlasting love
You in?

The Woman

I know some of the cost of discipleship
That more people will hate than love me
That those closest to me may turn away
And I will have nowhere to lay my head
But if I am with you, my life is complete

I have been at the margins before
Pushed out of every semi-safe place
And roasted in the heat of public opinion
You, too, have walked this road before
And it is my joy to meet you here

If you will send your presence before me
If you will put your words in my mouth
If you will saturate me in your love
My daily cross will be a light burden
To bear in this short section of eternity

The Beloved

Walk this way, My Delight
Put your feet in my footprints
For I will not ask you to walk
Anywhere I, myself, have not
Gone before

The Woman

My Beloved teaches me the way
In which I should walk

The Beloved

You are not what you think you are
I did not make you to be pushed around
To forever yield and morph to other's expectations

To find yourself always at their mercy

You are my glory on earth

The Woman

I am no longer afraid

Of the gaze that only sees the surface

Nor am I angry at the heart that longs

Only to splash in the tepid shallows

Of acquaintance without true knowledge

Because I, too, have been drawn to Beauty

Dazzling to my sight, weakening to my knees

A Beauty I can only know in part[1]

On this side of eternity

Therefore, the world's misconception of beauty

No longer devalues me where I stand

Nor will I blame myself

Regarding any man's violent battle for control

No, I am not to blame

For their misinterpretation of grace

My Beloved delights in my being

Every fiber of how I'm made

He loves

How, then, can I hate what he has called good?

1. 1 Corinthians 13:9–12

The Daughters of the Kingdom

How can we hate what he has called good?

She turns heads everywhere she walks

The Woman

Rest, O Daughters of the Kingdom!

Take a break from your vicious vigil

I am new among the ranks

And my love for the Lord is true

I strive to keep his commandments

And I live to do his work

I have no need for competition

Nor do I have any desire

For your married men

(to her Beloved)

They look on me with suspicion and disdain

Since I have caught so many eyes

But I have no man to call my own

The Daughters of the Kingdom

How is our King so taken with you, sister?

Tell us how you captured his heart

And by what charms you won his affection

The Woman

He made me and sees me
Therefore, he delights in me

The Beloved

Take heart, my love
I have you in the palm of my hand[2]
And if the world can't recognize
This gift I've given, do not fret
I have you in the palm of my hand
Where fear and misogyny can't own you
Jealousy cannot bring down your value
I've got you, My Delight
I've got you

The Woman

I do not despise this life you've given me
Nor do I regret having followed your commands
It has been my greatest desire to see you
First and only in my heart. However,
It is not by choice that I've yet to start a family

Even so, I choose you again, Lord
With all my heart

2. John 10:28–30

The Beloved

Be home in me
When you're kicked out
And when you wander

Find shelter beneath my wings[3]
If the elements bombard you

Lay back in my arms
When the way is too much[4]

When you are lost
And severely disoriented
Be found in me

The Woman

You are the only one, my Beloved
Greater, then, the chance to see you
Be my everything
Let the world's opinion waste away
In your presence, God
Renew my mind and heart

#

My soul longs for your presence

3. Psalm 91:4
4. 1 Kings 19:7

My bones cry out for your touch

I burn to burn brighter

Expand in me

Let my being enlarge to house you

I desire more

Take this from me, Lord

Alleviate this desire

I cannot bear it

The Beloved

Do not give me your desire

I delight for you to keep it

My joy is in your passion

Your fervor for closeness with me

Do not tear it out or stuff it down

Relate to me through it

And trust

The Woman

Teach me to trust you

For more than a precious moment

To open myself further

When we reach a sore spot

Enable me to rest in your love

To rejoice in our union

And to know that in your presence

I am truly free

Mutual Adoration

The Woman

My Lord is the King of kings
His kingdom has no end
Fire is his countenance[1]
Jewels are his hands and feet
His tongue is a double-edged sword[2]
His heart is a nest
Carefully woven and lined with feathers
Where he nurtures his young

#

Protective, strong, gentle
My Beloved encloses me
On every side, he's present
"Who can compare to this?"
He asks
I laugh
And breathe easy in his arms

1. Revelation 1:14
2. Revelation 1:16

(to her Beloved)

What shall we do, and where shall we go?

The Beloved

Anywhere, love, anywhere

Love's enjoyment is to be had in all the world

Come with me, my love

My Delight

The Woman

My Beloved is my vine

And I am his branches[3]

He is my everlasting source[4]

My rock and my redeemer[5]

He is my firm foundation

My solid ground[6]

He is the blood in my veins

The breath in my lungs

He is my mother and father

My brother, friend, and King

He is my beginning and my end[7]

My Beloved is mine

And I am his[8]

3. John 15:5
4. 1 Corinthians 8:5–6
5. Psalm 19:14
6. 2 Timothy 2:19
7. Revelation 21:6
8. Song of Solomon 2:16

The Beloved

This sweetness that envelopes us
This lovely, intoxicating fragrance
This thick, tangible love is your worship
For your words are sweet to me, my love
And your heart is precious
Lift your face to mine, linger,
And receive from me

The Woman

My Delight is his delight
And his pleasure is all mine
The joy of my King awakens my heart
And of my overflow I pour out to him
Again, he has come to fill me
And I am content
For we are one

(to her Beloved)

How can I ever leave this space
The warmth of your presence
The peace of your security
The joy of our union
I'll never get anything done
Only to dream of returning to my Love

The Beloved

Then, don't leave
I am with you wherever you go[9]
So, do not depart from my arms
Do not forget our love and union
Live in them
And abide in me[10]

The Woman

King of all kings
Love of all loves
My Beloved is
God of all gods
Worthiest, he is to me,
In me, treasure of all treasure
Peace of all peace
Fulfillment of all fulfillment

The Beloved

My Delight has been the desire of many men
Yet their eyes grow dark to her; their enthusiasm fades
Predictably so, for they are empty
See, here, how she seeks
Life in one who has
See, now, how she finds
Wholeness in a gaze that never wanders

9. Joshua 1:9
10. John 15:4

Safety in the grasp of hands that will not violate

Healing in the word that will not tear her down

She has found life in me, and rightly so

The Woman

You satisfy me just enough

To keep me longing for more

More of you

To know your character and thoughts

To delight my heart in yours

To find yet another aching space

For you to heal and fill

I am ruined, my King

Ruined and hungry

Only for your love

The Beloved

I desire you, my love

Not for what you can give me

Nor to elevate my self-regard

I want you with me

I made you and you are wonderful

Our relationship brings you life

And you bring me My Delight

The Woman

My passion in your hands

The Beloved

My passion in yours

The Woman

Tell me again and again
How much you love me
Yes, I remember when it hurt to hear
But what joy these words bring to me
Now that you've stretched me

Tell me again, tell me forever
And I will receive your love
Until I can receive no more
I bask in the light of your love
And you graciously astound me
By basking in mine

(to the Daughters of the Kingdom)

O sisters, rejoice at his heart!
He comes to me in my longing
The fragrance of our love hangs thickly in the air
His desire encompasses mine
And purifies it in grace and glory
He embraces me, yet he will not invade
His words waft over me and
As I give him entrance,
In and through me

We abide, I in him and he in me

\#

He's braided me in
A fourth strand to his three
A promise as he weaves me
In him, through him
Under him, over him
Around him, *in* him
We are together
Forever

The Beloved

My love has become like the wild flowers
That spring up after a desert flood
She is vibrant in beauty
And tender in the sunlight
Her glory covers the waste places
And brings refreshment to weary eyes
Blessed is the creation of my heart,
My beloved, My Delight

The Woman

We breathe each other in
For the enjoyment of love
I am embarrassed by this covenant
Which benefits me so disproportionately

He shakes his head and smiles

The Beloved

I am rich, my love
I am rich

The Woman

You are my exceedingly great reward![11]
How can it be that this love
Came to me, not by achievement
But by grace?
Through faith,[12] you remind me

This is not of me; it is all you
All you, my worthy Beloved

The Beloved

Hey, everyone, she *loves* me!
Let all of Heaven resound with music
Flutes and harps and cymbals
Electric guitar, why not?
She loves me, guys!

See how her heart brims
With joy at my voice
How she cranes her neck

11. Genesis 15:1
12. Ephesians 2:8-9

To get a glimpse of me

Every chance she gets

(to the Woman)

Look up, My Delight

Do not cast your gaze downward

This is the day of our hopes

The unfolding we've been waiting for

Call all the angels

Strike up the band

Let's dance all day and all night

It's time to celebrate

Our love

The Woman

To be in your presence

Is to want you more, my Beloved

To desire you is to live, ever-seeking,

Knowing I *shall* find you

The grace of having you

Is to find wholeness amidst the ruins

Of what I once thought was true life

No one understands a wall-less city

But you are a wall of fire about me

In me, you reveal your glory[13]

As we come up from the wilderness,

13. Zechariah 2:4–5

I will lean on you,[14] wait on you
Every step of the way
Surely, I will never walk alone

Come, my Lord and Love
In your faithfulness and strength
Transform your bride
In the light of your unfailing love
Come to me, my Beloved
I know that your desire is toward me[15]
Therefore, I will wait for you
In spirit and in truth[16]

14. Song of Solomon 8:5
15. Song of Solomon 7:10
16. John 4:24